SODA POP
Cookbook

Printed in the USA by G&R Publishing Co., Waverly, IA

Published and distributed by:

507 Industrial Street
Waverly, IA 50677

ISBN-13: 978-1-56383-371-7
ISBN-10: 1-56383-371-9
Item #3724

Beverages

Vanilla Cream

½ C. light cream
½ tsp. vanilla extract

½ tsp. sugar substitute
1½ C. Diet Vanilla Coke

In a small pitcher, combine 1 cup crushed ice, cream, vanilla and sugar substitute; stir to combine. Chill well. Divide mixture evenly between 2 chilled glasses. Add ¾ cup Diet Vanilla Coke to each glass; stir gently to combine. Makes 2 servings.

Melon Smoothie

2½ C. diced honeydew melon
2 T. chopped fresh mint
1 T. lime juice

Pinch of salt
⅓ C. ginger ale, chilled

In a blender container, combine melon, mint, lime juice, salt, ginger ale and 6 ice cubes. Process until smooth. Makes 2 servings.

Chocolate Fizz

½ C. chocolate syrup
2 C. milk*
24 oz. 7UP**, room temperature

Whipped topping, thawed, optional
Decorator sprinkles or nonpareils,
    optional

In a 4-cup glass measuring cup, stir together chocolate syrup and milk until well blended. Microwave uncovered on high power for 3 to 4 minutes, or until hot. Divide mixture evenly among 6 mugs. Slowly pour about ½ cup 7UP into each mug. Stir. Top with whipped topping and decorator sprinkles, if desired. Makes 6 servings.

*Try with chocolate milk.
**Try with Pepsi or Coca-Cola.

Mango Soda

½ lb. mango, peeled, pitted and
   coarsely chopped
¾ C. sugar
½ tsp. vanilla extract

Pinch of salt
2 T. orange juice
Club soda

In a food processor bowl, combine mango, sugar, vanilla and salt; process to puree. Blend in orange juice. Strain into a small pitcher; refrigerate until serving time. At serving time, mix mango mixture with club soda to desired strength. Makes 4 servings.

Flavored Cola

To make Cherry Cola:
¾ C. Coca-Cola
1 T. grenadine syrup
1 T. maraschino cherry juice

To make Vanilla Cola:
¾ C. Coca-Cola
¼ tsp. vanilla extract

To make Chocolate Cola:
¾ C. Coca-Cola
2 to 3 tsp. chocolate syrup

In a tall glass, combine Coca-Cola and flavorings; stir to blend. Add ice. Makes 1 serving.

Cola Freeze

1 (14 oz.) can sweetened
   condensed milk

12 oz. Coca-Cola

In a 4-cup measuring cup, blend together sweetened condensed milk and Coca-Cola. Pour into ice cube trays and freeze overnight. Place cubes in individual serving bowls. Makes 3 to 4 servings.

Pineapple Fizzy

1½ C. pineapple juice*   ½ C. club soda
1 C. pineapple sherbet**

In a blender container, blend pineapple juice, sherbet and club soda until smooth.
Makes 2 servings.

*Try with orange juice.
**Try with orange sherbet.

White Grape Cooler

2 (12 oz.) cans frozen apple juice
concentrate, thawed

2 (11.5 oz.) cans frozen white grape
juice concentrate, thawed

12 C. Sprite, chilled

Lemon slices, optional

Lime slices, optional

In a large pitcher or punch bowl, mix together apple and white grape juice concentrates. Stir in 6 cups cold water. Chill until serving time. Add Sprite; stir to combine. Garnish with lemon and lime slices, if desired. Makes 20 to 24 servings.

Tip: For festive ice cubes, place grapes in ice cube trays and cover with white grape juice or water. Freeze.

Orange Slush

2 C. sugar
1 (16 oz.) can frozen lemonade
    concentrate, thawed

1 (12 oz.) can frozen orange juice
    concentrate, thawed
4¼ C. ginger ale, chilled

In a 5-quart plastic ice cream bucket or other comparably sized freezer-safe container with a lid, dissolve sugar in 9 cups hot water. Stir in lemonade concentrate and orange juice concentrate. Freeze for 8 to 10 hours; stir. Keep in the freezer until ready to serve. At serving time, fill glass ⅔ full with slush; finish filling with ginger ale. Stir. Makes 16 servings.

Apple Orchard Punch

32 oz. apple juice, chilled
1 (12 oz.) can frozen cranberry juice
   cocktail concentrate, thawed

1 C. orange juice
1½ qts. ginger ale, chilled
1 red apple

In a large punch bowl, combine apple juice, cranberry concentrate and orange juice; stir to blend well. Slowly add ginger ale. Slice apple horizontally; remove seeds and float in punch bowl. Makes 3 quarts.

Red Cream Soda Punch

2 (12 oz.) cans frozen orange juice
concentrate, thawed
1 (12 oz.) can frozen lemonade
concentrate, thawed

½ C. sugar
2 liters red cream soda, chilled

In a punch bowl, combine 4 quarts cold water, orange juice concentrate, lemonade concentrate and sugar. Stir until sugar is dissolved. Refrigerate for 2 hours or until chilled. Stir in red cream soda just before serving. Makes 28 servings.

Mock Champagne Punch

¾ C. sugar
1 C. grapefruit juice
½ C. orange juice
½ C. grenadine syrup

1½ C. ginger ale, chilled
Twists of lemon peel, optional
Maraschino cherries with stems,
   optional

In a small saucepan over low heat, combine sugar and 1 cup water. Simmer about 1 minute or until sugar is dissolved, stirring constantly. In a 2-quart non-metal pitcher, mix grapefruit juice, orange juice and grenadine syrup. Add sugar mixture; stir to combine. Refrigerate. Just before serving, add ginger ale and ice; stir gently. Garnish with lemon twists and cherries, if desired. Makes 4 to 5 servings.

Sherbet Punch

2 liters 7UP, chilled   2 liters ginger ale, chilled
1 gal. sherbet, any flavor, slightly
    softened

In a punch bowl, mix 7UP and sherbet until thickened. Stir in ginger ale just before serving. Makes 20 to 24 servings.

Banana Punch

1 (16 oz.) bag frozen strawberries, partially thawed
1 (16 oz.) can crushed pineapple
3 bananas, peeled and sliced

½ gal. apple-strawberry juice drink
4 C. Coca-Cola
½ gal. vanilla ice cream, softened

In a blender container, combine ⅓ each of the strawberries, pineapple and bananas. Add about ¼ of the juice drink. Blend on low speed until well mixed. Pour mixture into a punch bowl. Repeat twice. Pour remainder of juice drink and Coca-Cola into punch bowl; stir. Carefully scoop ice cream into punch bowl and stir to blend ice cream. Makes 20 to 24 servings.

Cinnamon Wassail

1 gal. apple cider
2 liters 7UP
24 whole cloves

2 cinnamon sticks
½ C. red-hot cinnamon candies

In a large saucepan over medium heat, heat apple cider, 7UP, cloves and cinnamon until hot. Add candies, stirring constantly until melted. Remove cloves and cinnamon sticks. Serve hot. Makes 18 to 20 servings.

Mint Julep

1½ C. sugar
1 bunch fresh mint

1 C. lemon juice
2 liters ginger ale

In a medium saucepan over medium heat, boil 1½ cups water and sugar for 5 minutes, stirring constantly. Remove from heat. Stir in mint and lemon juice. To a large pitcher, add ice and ginger ale. Stir in mint mixture. Serve over ice in tall glasses. Makes 8 to 10 servings.

Kiddie Cocktail

1 C. 7UP
2 T. grenadine syrup
1 T. orange juice

1 lemon slice
1 maraschino cherry

Fill a tall glass with ice cubes. Add 7UP, grenadine syrup and orange juice; stir to combine. Garnish with lemon slice and cherry. Makes 1 serving.

Mock Margarita

½ C. orange-tangerine juice blend, chilled
½ C. limeade, chilled
½ C. lemonade, chilled
Juice of 1 lime
Juice of 1 lemon
Zest of ½ lemon
½ orange, peeled and quartered
Pinch of salt
¼ C. kosher salt, optional

In a blender container, combine juice blend, limeade, lemonade, lime juice, lemon juice, lemon zest, orange, salt and ½ cup crushed ice. Blend on high speed for 3 to 5 minutes or until slushy. Coat the rim of two margarita glasses with lime juice and press into kosher salt, if desired. Pour slush mixture into prepared glasses. Makes 2 servings.

Breads & Jellies
Pepsi Pancakes

1½ C. flour
3 T. sugar
1 T. baking powder
¼ tsp. salt
Pinch of ground nutmeg

2 eggs, room temperature
1¼ C. Pepsi, room temperature
½ tsp. vanilla extract
3 T. butter plus more if needed

In a large bowl, stir together flour, sugar, baking powder, salt and nutmeg. In a medium bowl, beat eggs; whisk in Pepsi and vanilla. In a large heavy skillet or griddle over medium heat, melt butter. Pour melted butter into Pepsi mixture. Combine Pepsi mixture and dry ingredients, whisking until batter is just thick. Keeping the skillet at medium heat, ladle about ¼ cup batter into skillet for each pancake, keeping space between each. Cook until bubbles form on the surface of pancakes and the bottoms are golden brown, about 2 minutes. Flip and cook about 1 minute more or until bottoms are golden brown. Serve immediately or transfer to a platter and cover loosely with foil to keep warm. Repeat with remaining batter, adding more butter to skillet as needed. Makes 4 servings.

French Toast With Vanilla Syrup

3 C. Vanilla Coca-Cola
1½ T. butter, divided
16 pecan halves
2 tsp. sugar
Pinch of salt

1 egg
3 egg whites
¼ C. milk
½ tsp. ground cinnamon, optional
1 (1 lb.) loaf egg bread, cut into ½" slices

Spray a baking sheet with nonstick cooking spray; set aside. In a medium saucepan over medium-high heat, bring Coca-Cola to a boil. Reduce heat to low and simmer for 25 to 30 minutes or until reduced to ⅔ cup. Add 1½ teaspoons butter and simmer, whisking occasionally until syrup is reduced to ½ cup. Remove from heat and keep warm. In a small nonstick skillet over medium heat, stir pecans for 5 minutes or until pecans begin to brown. Remove from heat and add remaining 1 tablespoon butter; stir to coat pecans. Return pan to heat and sprinkle pecans with sugar and salt. Cook and stir for 2 to 4 minutes or until a light caramel glaze forms. Remove from heat and pour pecans onto prepared baking sheet; cool. Meanwhile, in a shallow

continued on next page

bowl, whisk together egg, egg whites, milk and cinnamon, if desired. Spray a large nonstick skillet with nonstick cooking spray and heat over medium heat. Working in batches, dip both sides of bread slices in egg mixture until coated, draining excess. Place in hot skillet and cook for 2 to 3 minutes on one side or until light golden brown; flip and cook the other side until light golden brown. Remove from skillet and keep warm. Repeat with remaining bread slices. Serve French toast with Coca-Cola syrup and glazed pecans, breaking pecans apart if necessary. Makes 4 servings.

Rise & Shine Muffins

1 C. quick-cooking oats
½ C. whole wheat flour
½ C. flour
½ tsp. salt
¾ C. egg substitute
1 C. sugar
½ C. unsweetened applesauce

2 T. canola oil
¾ C. Coca-Cola
1½ tsp. vanilla extract
2 C. finely grated carrots
½ C. finely grated zucchini
½ C. raisins
¼ C. chopped nuts, optional

Preheat oven to 350°. Place paper liners in a muffin pan(s); set aside. In a small bowl, mix together oats, whole wheat flour, flour and salt. In a large bowl, whisk together egg substitute, sugar, applesauce, oil, Coca-Cola and vanilla. Gently fold dry ingredients into wet ingredients. Fold in carrots, zucchini, raisins and nuts, if desired, just until combined. Spoon batter into liners and bake for 20 minutes. Makes 12 to 18 muffins.

Simple Pumpkin Muffins

1 (18.2 oz.) pkg. spice cake mix
   (without pudding)

1 (15 oz.) can pumpkin puree
½ C. Mellow Yellow

Preheat oven to 350°. Place paper liners in two muffin pans; set aside. In a large bowl, combine cake mix, pumpkin puree and Mellow Yellow, stirring until well combined. Spoon batter into liners and bake for 15 to 20 minutes or until a toothpick inserted in the center of a muffin comes out clean. Makes 18 to 20 muffins.

Kiwifruit Muffins

1 C. flour
½ C. sugar
½ tsp. baking soda
½ tsp. ground cinnamon
¼ tsp. ground allspice
Pinch of salt

1 egg
½ C. 7UP
2 T. butter, melted
2 kiwifruit, peeled and chopped
½ C. raisins

Preheat oven to 425°. Place paper liners in a muffin pan; set aside. In a medium bowl, combine flour, sugar, baking soda, cinnamon, allspice and salt; stir to blend. In a small bowl, combine egg, 7UP and butter; beat until well mixed. Add egg mixture to dry ingredients and stir just until moistened. Fold in kiwifruit and raisins. Spoon batter into liners and bake for 15 to 18 minutes or until a toothpick inserted in the center of a muffin comes out clean. Makes 12 muffins.

Sour Cream 7UP Biscuits

4 C. biscuit mix   ¾ C. 7UP
1 C. sour cream

Preheat oven to 400°. Grease a baking sheet; set aside. In a large bowl, mix together biscuit mix and sour cream with a pastry blender or two knives until mixture is crumbly. Add 7UP, stirring quickly with a large fork. Turn dough onto a lightly floured surface and quickly knead 6 to 8 times. Do not overmix. Pat into an 8″ square. Using a knife dipped in flour, cut into 16 equal-sized squares, or use a 2″ biscuit cutter and cut into rounds. Place biscuits 2″ apart on prepared baking sheet. Bake for 10 to 20 minutes or until golden brown. Makes 16 servings.

Coca-Cola Banana Bread

2½ C. brown sugar
½ C. vegetable oil
4 eggs
2 tsp. vanilla extract
1 to 2 tsp. ground cinnamon
¼ tsp. ground cloves
2 tsp. baking powder

¼ tsp. salt
3¼ C. flour
2 C. mashed, ripe bananas
1 C. Coca-Cola
1 C. miniature semi-sweet chocolate
    chips, optional
1 C. chopped walnuts, optional

Preheat oven to 300°. Grease two 5 x 9″ loaf pans; set aside. In a large bowl, mix together brown sugar, oil, eggs and vanilla. In a medium bowl, sift together cinnamon, cloves, baking powder, salt and flour. Stir dry ingredients into brown sugar mixture. Add bananas and Coca-Cola, stirring to combine. Fold in chocolate chips and walnuts, if desired. Divide batter evenly among prepared pans. Set pans on a baking sheet or jellyroll pan. Bake for 1 hour 20 minutes to 1 hour 30 minutes or until a toothpick inserted in center of bread comes out clean. Makes 2 loaves.

Easy Orange Bread

3 C. self-rising flour*
2 T. sugar

12 oz. orange soda, room temperature

Preheat oven to 375°. Grease a 5 x 9″ loaf pan; set aside. In a large bowl, combine flour, sugar and orange soda, stirring until well combined. Pour mixture into prepared pan. Bake for 45 minutes or until a toothpick inserted in center of bread comes out clean. Makes 1 loaf.

Or substitute 3 cups all-purpose flour mixed with 3 teaspoons baking powder, 1½ teaspoons salt and ¾ teaspoon baking soda for the self-rising flour.

Date Nut Bread

1¼ C. Coca-Cola
1 (8 oz.) pkg. pitted dates, chopped
1 C. brown sugar
2 T. vegetable oil
2 C. flour

1 tsp. baking powder
1 tsp. baking soda
1 egg, beaten
1 tsp. vanilla extract
½ C. chopped pecans or walnuts

Preheat oven to 350°. Grease and flour a 5 x 9˝ loaf pan; set aside. In a medium saucepan over medium heat, bring Coca-Cola to a boil. Remove from heat and stir in dates, mixing well. Stir in brown sugar and oil; cool. In a large bowl, stir together flour, baking powder and baking soda. Add to date mixture, mixing thoroughly. Stir in egg, vanilla and pecans. Pour mixture into prepared pan. Bake for 1 hour or until a toothpick inserted in center of bread comes out clean. Set pan on a wire rack to cool for 20 minutes. Remove bread from pan; allow to cool on a wire rack, top side up. Refrigerate overnight before slicing. Makes 1 loaf.

Homemade Dr. Pepper Jelly

3½ C. sugar
¼ C. lemon juice
2¼ C. Dr. Pepper

Red food coloring, optional
3 oz. liquid fruit pectin

In a large saucepan over high heat, stir together sugar, lemon juice and Dr. Pepper. Add a few drops of food coloring, if desired. Bring to a boil, stirring constantly. Stir in pectin. Bring to a full boil and boil for 2 minutes. Remove from heat and skim off foam with a metal spoon. Pour into 8 (4-ounce) hot, sterilized jars, leaving ¼" headspace. Cover immediately with lids and process in boiling water bath for 6 minutes. Remove jars and cool to room temperature. When lids have sealed, store in a cool, dry place. Allow to set several days before serving. Use promptly after opening. Makes about 4 cups.

Mountain Dew Hot Jelly

2¾ C. Mountain Dew
2 T. lemon juice
½ C. minced fresh yellow hot peppers

1 C. apple cider vinegar
4½ C. sugar
1 (1.75 oz.) pkg. powdered fruit pectin

In a blender container, combine Mountain Dew, lemon juice, hot peppers and vinegar. Puree for about 2 minutes or until smooth. Pour mixture into a large nonreactive saucepan. Bring to a full rolling boil over medium heat. Slowly add sugar, stirring constantly until dissolved. Add fruit pectin, stirring to dissolve; adjust heat to maintain rolling boil for 1 minute. Remove from heat and skim off foam with a metal spoon. Pour into 12 (4-ounce) hot, sterilized jars, leaving ¼″ headspace. Cover immediately with lids and process in boiling water bath for 6 minutes. Remove jars and cool to room temperature. When lids have sealed, store in a cool, dry place. Use promptly after opening. Makes about 6 cups.

Salads & Sides

Frosted Cranberry Squares

1 (16 oz.) can crushed pineapple,
drained, juice reserved
1 (6 oz.) pkg. cherry gelatin
1 C. Coca-Cola
1 (14 oz.) can cranberry sauce

1 (8 oz.) pkg. cream cheese, softened
1 (8 oz.) container whipped topping,
thawed
1 C. chopped pecans

In a medium saucepan over medium heat, combine 1 cup reserved pineapple juice (adding water to make 1 cup, if necessary) and gelatin, stirring until gelatin is dissolved. Slowly add Coca-Cola, stirring to mix well. Pour into a medium bowl and refrigerate until mixture is slightly thickened. Stir in pineapple and cranberry sauce; refrigerate until set. In a medium mixing bowl, beat cream cheese on medium speed with an electric mixer until smooth. Stir in whipped topping. Spread cream cheese mixture over gelatin and sprinkle with pecans. Makes 6 to 8 servings.

Mountain Dew Salad

1 (.3 oz.) pkg. orange sugar-free gelatin
1 (.3 oz.) pkg. lemon sugar-free gelatin
20 oz. Diet Mountain Dew, divided
1 (8 oz.) can crushed pineapple, undrained
1 (11 oz.) can mandarin oranges, drained
2 medium bananas, peeled and diced

1 (.9 oz.) pkg. vanilla sugar-free instant pudding mix
⅔ C. nonfat dry milk powder
1 (8 oz.) pkg. fat-free cream cheese
1 C. fat-free whipped topping, thawed
1 tsp. coconut flavoring
½ C. miniature marshmallows
½ C. sweetened flaked coconut

In a large bowl, stir together orange and lemon gelatin. Add 1¼ cups boiling water; stir to dissolve. Stir in 1 cup Diet Mountain Dew, pineapple, mandarin oranges and bananas. Pour mixture into an 8 x 8″ dish; refrigerate. In a medium bowl, stir together pudding mix and dry milk powder. Whisk in remaining 1½ cups Diet Mountain Dew. Spread mixture evenly over firm gelatin mixture; refrigerate. In a medium bowl, beat cream cheese on medium speed with an electric mixer until smooth. Fold in whipped topping, coconut flavoring and marshmallows. Spread over pudding layer. Sprinkle with coconut. Refrigerate for at least 30 minutes. Makes 8 servings.

Frosty Lemon Fruit Salad

1 (6 oz.) pkg. lemon gelatin
2 C. ginger ale
1 (20 oz.) can crushed pineapple,
    drained, juice reserved
2 bananas, peeled and sliced

1 C. miniature marshmallows
2 T. flour
½ C. sugar
1 C. whipped topping, thawed
½ C. grated American cheese

In a large bowl, dissolve gelatin in 2 cups boiling water. Add ginger ale and refrigerate until partially set. Add pineapple, bananas and marshmallows. Pour into a 9 x 13″ pan; refrigerate until set. In a small saucepan, mix together flour and sugar. Add reserved pineapple juice (adding water to make 1 cup, if necessary) and cook over medium heat until thick; cool. Stir in whipped topping and spread over gelatin mixture in pan. Sprinkle with cheese. Refrigerate for 24 hours. Makes 20 servings.

Pepsi Salad

1 (6 oz.) pkg. cherry gelatin
12 oz. Diet Pepsi, chilled
1 (21 oz.) can cherry pie filling

1 (8 oz.) container whipped topping,
    thawed

In a large bowl, combine gelatin and 2 cups boiling water. Whisk to dissolve gelatin. Whisk in Diet Pepsi. Refrigerate until slightly thickened. Stir in pie filling and whipped topping. Makes 8 servings.

Dr. Pepper Freeze

1 (8 oz.) pkg. cream cheese, softened
⅓ C. Dr. Pepper
1 (11 oz.) can mandarin oranges,
    drained

1 (10 oz.) jar maraschino cherries,
    drained and halved
1 (20 oz.) can pineapple chunks,
    drained
1 C. miniature marshmallows

In a small mixing bowl, blend cream cheese with an electric mixer on medium speed until smooth. Slowly add Dr. Pepper, beating until creamy. Fold in mandarin oranges, cherries, pineapple and marshmallows. Spread evenly into an 8 x 8″ pan and freeze. Makes 9 servings.

Coca-Cola Salad

1 (20 oz.) can pineapple chunks,
   drained, juice reserved
1 (15 oz.) can bing cherries, drained,
   juice reserved
2 (3 oz.) pkgs. cherry gelatin

12 oz. Coca-Cola
3 (8 oz.) pkgs. cream cheese, softened
   and cubed
½ C. chopped pecans

In a medium saucepan over medium heat, combine 1½ cups reserved pineapple juice and cherry juice (adding water to make 1½ cups if necessary) and gelatin, stirring until gelatin is dissolved. Stir in Coca-Cola. Add cream cheese, whisking until well blended and smooth. Stir in pineapple, cherries and pecans. Pour into a medium bowl and refrigerate until firm. Makes 8 servings.

Slow-Cooker Applesauce

5 lbs. apples, peeled, cut into chunks, and seeded
12 oz. ginger ale

Ground cinnamon, optional
Brown sugar, optional

Place prepared apples in a 4-quart slow cooker. Pour ginger ale over apples and cook on low setting for 6 to 8 hours or until apples are soft. Remove from slow cooker and sprinkle with cinnamon and brown sugar, if desired. Makes 10 to 15 servings.

Pinto Beans

1 lb. dry pinto beans
½ C. chopped red bell pepper
2 tsp. chili powder
2 tsp. salt

1 bay leaf
½ tsp. dry mustard
12 oz. Coca-Cola

Spray a slow cooker with nonstick cooking spray. Add beans, bell pepper, chili powder, salt, bay leaf, dry mustard and Coca-Cola; stir to combine. Cook on low setting for 6 to 8 hours or until beans are tender. Remove bay leaf. Makes 6 to 8 servings.

Patio Bean Dish

3 (15 oz.) cans pork and beans
¾ C. Dr. Pepper
¼ C. ketchup

1 T. prepared mustard
1 onion, chopped
4 strips bacon

Preheat oven to 350°. Spray a 2-quart casserole dish with nonstick cooking spray; set aside. In a large bowl, stir together pork and beans, Dr. Pepper, ketchup, mustard and onion. Pour into prepared dish. Cut bacon into 2" pieces and arrange on top of bean mixture. Bake for 1½ to 2 hours. Makes 10 to 12 servings.

Root Beer Baked Beans

2 strips bacon, chopped
1 onion, chopped
2 (16 oz.) cans baked beans
½ C. root beer (not diet)

¼ C. barbeque sauce
½ tsp. dry mustard
Hot pepper sauce to taste
Black pepper to taste

In a large skillet over medium heat, fry bacon and onion until bacon is brown and crisp; drain. Add baked beans, root beer, barbeque sauce, dry mustard, hot pepper sauce and black pepper. Bring to a boil. Reduce heat and simmer, stirring often, for 20 minutes or until slightly thickened. Makes 4 to 6 servings.

Greek Style Green Beans

2 cloves garlic, minced
¼ C. chopped fresh parsley
2 T. sugar
2 tsp. dried oregano
2 tsp. prepared mustard
½ tsp. salt

½ C. Coca-Cola
¼ C. olive oil
2 T. balsamic vinegar
2 shallots or small onions
2 (14.5 oz.) cans small, whole green
    beans, drained

In a large bowl, whisk together garlic, parsley, sugar, oregano, mustard, salt, Coca-Cola, oil and vinegar until sugar is dissolved. Peel and thinly slice shallots; separate into rings. Add shallots and beans to Coca-Cola mixture; toss lightly. Cover and refrigerate overnight. Serve hot or cold. Makes 4 to 6 servings.

Dr. Squash

1 acorn squash, halved
1 T. butter
Pinch of ground cinnamon, optional

1½ tsp. brown sugar
12 oz. Dr. Pepper

Preheat oven to 350°. Remove seeds and fibers from squash. Using crumpled aluminum foil, make rings to hold each squash half upright. Set foil rings on a jellyroll pan. Set squash halves on rings, cut side up. Rub 1½ teaspoons butter in the cavity of each squash half. In a small bowl, stir together cinnamon and brown sugar. Sprinkle over butter. Pour Dr. Pepper into each cavity to fill. Bake for 30 to 60 minutes or until squash is soft. Makes 2 servings.

Root Beer'd Sweet Potatoes

32 oz. root beer
1 C. bourbon*
2 T. lemon juice

¼ C. butter
Pinch of ground cloves
⅓ C. cornstarch

In a medium saucepan over medium heat, combine root beer, bourbon, lemon juice, butter and cloves; bring to a boil. In a small bowl, combine cornstarch and ¾ cup water; stir to dissolve and add to bourbon mixture. Serve over sliced boiled sweet potatoes. Makes 6 cups.

Or substitute 3 tablespoons vanilla extract (adding water to make 1 cup) for the bourbon.

Lemon-Lime Glazed Carrots

1 onion, chopped
2 T. butter
1½ lbs. carrots, thinly sliced

1 C. 7UP
Salt and black pepper to taste
1 T. sugar

In a large saucepan over medium heat, sauté onion in butter. Add carrots and 7UP. Season to taste with salt and black pepper. Add sugar and cook over high heat for 8 to 10 minutes or until liquid is absorbed and carrots are lightly glazed. Makes 6 servings.

Marinades & Sauces

Dr. Pepper Glaze

12 oz. Dr. Pepper
1½ C. brown sugar
¼ C. orange juice

4 tsp. Dijon mustard
Pinch of ground cloves
½ tsp. ground nutmeg

In a medium nonreactive saucepan over medium heat, whisk together Dr. Pepper, brown sugar, orange juice and Dijon mustard; bring to a boil. Reduce heat to medium-low and simmer for 8 minutes or until mixture is thickened; let cool. Add cloves and nutmeg. Use to glaze ham. Makes 3¼ cups.

Zippy Lime & Jalapeño Glaze

1 C. Coca-Cola
¼ C. lime juice
2 C. brown sugar

2 jalapeño peppers, seeded and
thinly sliced

In a small nonreactive saucepan over medium heat, whisk together Coca-Cola, lime juice, brown sugar and jalapeño peppers. Bring to a boil. Reduce heat to a simmer and continue cooking until mixture becomes syrupy, about 6 minutes. Use to glaze ham or chicken. Makes 3 cups.

Dr. Pepper BBQ Sauce

2½ C. Dr. Pepper
1 C. ketchup
½ C. vegetable oil
½ C. lemon juice
¼ C. dry minced onion

2 tsp. salt
1 tsp. garlic powder
1 tsp. black pepper
1 tsp. dried basil
¼ tsp. ground cayenne pepper

In a blender container, combine Dr. Pepper, ketchup, oil, lemon juice, onion, salt, garlic powder, black pepper, basil and cayenne pepper. Blend until well combined. Refrigerate in a tightly sealed container. Shake well before using with your favorite meat. Makes 5 cups.

Coca-Cola Style BBQ Sauce

1 onion, chopped
1 C. ketchup
1 C. Coca-Cola
2 tsp. Worcestershire sauce

2 tsp. molasses or brown sugar
2 tsp. distilled white vinegar
2 tsp. prepared mustard

In a medium bowl, stir together onion, ketchup, Coca-Cola, Worcestershire sauce, molasses, vinegar and mustard. Use with your favorite meat. Makes 3¼ cups.

Drunken Root Beer BBQ Sauce

½ C. olive oil
1 medium onion, chopped
2 ancho peppers
5 Roma tomatoes, quartered
5 cloves garlic

½ C. prepared mustard
½ C. tomato puree
2 C. root beer
2 C. beer
½ C. chopped fresh cilantro

Heat olive oil in a medium nonreactive saucepan over medium heat; add onion, ancho peppers, tomatoes and garlic. Cook for 3 minutes. Add mustard, tomato puree, root beer, beer and cilantro; bring to a boil. Reduce heat to low; simmer for 45 minutes or until slightly thickened. Pour sauce into a blender container and process until smooth. Use with your favorite meat. Makes 3 cups.

Cola Steak Marinade

20 oz. Coca-Cola
¾ C. canola oil
¼ C. chopped green onion
⅓ C. chopped yellow onion
¼ C. chopped fresh cilantro
1 jalapeño pepper, seeded and chopped

1 clove garlic, finely chopped
1 tsp. crushed red pepper flakes
½ tsp. salt
1 tsp. ground cumin
¼ tsp. black pepper
Juice and zest of 2 limes

In a medium bowl, stir together Coca-Cola, oil, green and yellow onions, cilantro, jalapeño pepper, garlic, red pepper flakes, salt, cumin, black pepper, lime juice and lime zest. Use to marinate steak. Makes 4½ cups.

Root Beer Teriyaki Marinade

2 C. root beer
1 C. soy sauce
1 T. ground ginger

1 T. garlic powder
Black pepper to taste

In a medium nonreactive saucepan over medium heat, whisk together root beer, soy sauce, ginger, garlic powder and black pepper; heat until warm but not boiling. Use to marinate beef or chicken. Makes 3 cups.

Soups & Main Dishes

French Onion Soup

¼ C. butter
4 C. thinly sliced onions
2 (10.5 oz.) cans beef broth
¾ C. Coca-Cola, room temperature
1 tsp. salt

½ tsp. white wine vinegar
Pinch of black pepper
8 thick-cut slices French bread
Grated Parmesan cheese

In a large saucepan over medium heat, melt butter; add onions and cook, stirring occasionally until light golden brown. Add broth, 1 soup can water, Coca-Cola, salt, vinegar and black pepper. Reduce heat. Cover and simmer for 20 to 25 minutes. On a broiler pan, toast one side of French bread slices until light golden brown. Turn and generously sprinkle with Parmesan cheese; toast the other side until light golden brown. Ladle soup into individual serving bowls and top each with 2 pieces of toast, cheese side up. Makes 4 servings.

Chili

1½ lbs. ground beef
1 (10.5 oz.) can French onion soup
2 tsp. ground cumin
2 (15 oz.) cans chili beans
10 oz. Coca-Cola

½ tsp. salt
1 T. chili powder
½ tsp. black pepper
1 (8 oz.) can tomato sauce
1 (6 oz.) can tomato paste

In a large saucepan over medium heat, brown ground beef until no longer pink; drain. Add soup, cumin, chili beans, Coca-Cola, salt, chili powder, black pepper, tomato sauce and tomato paste; stir to combine well. Reduce heat to low and simmer until heated through. Makes 4 to 6 servings.

Beef Stew

3 T. shortening
3 lbs. stew beef
3 tsp. salt
1 tsp. black pepper
¼ C. flour
2 C. beef stock

2 C. Dr. Pepper
2 C. sliced carrots
1½ C. chopped onion
1 C. sliced celery
1 C. frozen peas

Heat shortening in a large saucepan over medium heat. Sprinkle stew beef with salt and black pepper and dust with flour. Brown stew beef on all sides in hot shortening. Drain off excess liquid. Add beef stock, Dr. Pepper, carrots, onion and celery; reduce heat to low. Cover and cook for 2½ to 3 hours or until meat is very tender. Add frozen peas in the last 10 minutes of cooking time. Makes 8 servings.

Grilled Burgers

1 egg	2 T. grated Parmesan cheese
½ C. Pepsi, divided	¼ tsp. salt
½ C. crushed soda crackers	1½ lbs. ground beef
6 T. French dressing, divided	6 hamburger buns

In a large bowl, stir together egg, ¼ cup Pepsi, crushed crackers, 2 tablespoons dressing, cheese and salt. Add ground beef and mix well. Shape mixture into 6 patties; set aside. In a small bowl, combine remaining ¼ cup Pepsi and 4 tablespoons dressing. Lightly grease grill grate and preheat grill to medium heat. Grill patties, uncovered, for 3 minutes on each side. Brush with Pepsi mixture; grill for 8 to 10 minutes longer or until juices run clear, basting and turning as needed. Serve on hamburger buns. Makes 6 servings.

Goulash

3 lbs. lean beef chuck roast
2 T. vegetable oil
2 C. chopped onion
1 clove garlic, minced
1 T. paprika
2½ tsp. salt

½ tsp. caraway seed
½ C. Coca-Cola
¼ C. red wine
4 tomatoes, chopped
3 T. flour
1 (16 oz.) pkg. noodles

Cut roast into ½″ cubes. In a large Dutch oven or saucepan, heat oil. Add meat, stirring to brown all sides. Remove roast. In the same pan, sauté onion and garlic until soft. Stir in paprika, salt and caraway seed; cook for 1 minute. Stir in roast, Coca-Cola, wine and tomatoes. Cover pan tightly and simmer for 1½ hours or until meat is fork-tender. In a small bowl, blend together flour and a small amount of water to make a smooth paste; stir into goulash. Cook noodles according to package directions. Serve meat mixture with hot noodles. Makes 8 servings.

Spaghetti & Meat Sauce

1 (16 oz.) pkg. spaghetti
2 lbs. ground beef
1 C. chopped onion
½ tsp. garlic powder
½ tsp. Italian seasoning
½ tsp. salt

½ tsp. black pepper
12 oz. Dr. Pepper
1 (15 oz.) can tomato sauce
2 T. Worcestershire sauce
1½ C. shredded mozzarella cheese

Preheat oven to 350°. Spray a 9 x 13″ baking pan with nonstick cooking spray; set aside. In a large saucepan, cook spaghetti according to package directions; drain and set aside. In a large Dutch oven or skillet over medium heat, brown ground beef; drain well. To ground beef in skillet, add onion, garlic powder, Italian seasoning, salt and black pepper. Cook for 5 minutes. Add Dr. Pepper, tomato sauce and Worcestershire sauce; cook for an additional 5 minutes. Stir in cooked spaghetti and cheese. Pour spaghetti mixture into prepared pan and bake for 20 to 30 minutes. Makes 8 servings.

Sloppy Joes

1 lb. ground beef
1 medium onion, chopped
1½ T. flour
1 C. Coca-Cola
⅔ C. ketchup

2 T. distilled white vinegar
1 T. Worcestershire sauce
2 tsp. dry mustard
8 hamburger buns

In a large skillet over medium heat, combine ground beef and onion. Cook, stirring occasionally, until beef is no longer pink and onions are tender; drain. Stir in flour, Coca-Cola, ketchup, vinegar, Worcestershire sauce and dry mustard until well combined. Reduce heat; cover and simmer for 30 minutes. Serve on hamburger buns. Makes 8 servings.

Sweet & Sour Meatballs

2 lbs. ground beef
1 potato, grated
½ C. uncooked rice
1 onion, minced

1 egg
2 C. ketchup
2 C. ginger ale

In a large bowl, mix together ground beef, grated potato, rice, onion and egg until well combined. Form meat mixture into 2″ balls. In a large saucepan over medium heat, combine ketchup and ginger ale; bring to a boil. Reduce heat to a simmer. Place meat balls into liquid; cover and cook for 1 hour. Makes 6 to 8 servings.

BBQ Brisket

6 lbs. beef brisket, trimmed
12 oz. Coca-Cola
1 C. chili sauce

1 (1 oz.) pkg. dry onion soup mix
2 C. barbeque sauce

Preheat oven to 300°. Spray a roasting pan with nonstick cooking spray. Place brisket in prepared pan. In a medium bowl, stir together Coca-Cola, chili sauce and soup mix; pour over brisket in pan. Cover and bake for 3 hours. Add barbeque sauce and return to oven until barbeque sauce is hot and brisket is cooked to desired doneness. Makes 10 to 12 servings.

Italian Brisket

3 to 4 lbs. beef brisket, trimmed
1 (16 oz.) bottle Italian salad dressing

16 oz. Coca-Cola

Place brisket in a deep bowl. In a medium bowl, whisk together salad dressing and Coca-Cola. Pour mixture over brisket, adding more cola to cover, if necessary. Refrigerate for 24 hours. Preheat oven to 200°. Place meat and marinade into a roasting pan; cover and bake for 6 to 8 hours or until meat is cooked to desired doneness. Makes 4 to 6 servings.

BBQ Steak

6 T. plus 2 tsp. ketchup
2 T. Diet Coke
1 T. brown sugar
1 T. cider vinegar
1 tsp. Worcestershire sauce

1 tsp. chili powder
½ clove garlic, minced
Ground cayenne pepper to taste
2 (7 oz.) beef steaks, trimmed

In a small saucepan over medium-high heat, whisk together ketchup, Diet Coke, brown sugar, vinegar, Worcestershire sauce, chili powder, garlic and cayenne pepper. Bring to a boil; reduce heat to low and simmer, stirring occasionally, for 20 minutes or until thickened. Remove from heat; cool to room temperature. Pierce both sides of steak with a fork. In a shallow baking dish, pour sauce over steak. Turn to coat both sides of steak. Cover and refrigerate overnight, turning occasionally. Preheat broiler. Remove steaks from sauce and place on broiler pan. Broil 4″ from the heat for 4 to 8 minutes on each side or to desired doneness, brushing with remaining sauce. Makes 2 servings.

Steak Kebabs

2 lbs. beef sirloin steaks   3 cloves garlic, minced
1 T. Creole seasoning   1 C. Coca-Cola

Cut steaks into 1″ thick strips. In a 9 x 13″ glass dish, arrange steak strips in a single layer and sprinkle with Creole seasoning and garlic. Pour Coca-Cola over seasoned steak and toss lightly. Marinate for 30 to 60 minutes. Lightly grease grill grate and preheat grill to medium heat. Thread seasoned meat onto metal or wooden* skewers. Grill kebabs for 4 to 6 minutes on each side or to desired doneness, basting with remaining marinade. Makes 4 to 6 servings.

*If using wooden skewers, be sure to soak in water at least 30 minutes to prevent burning.

Beef Sandwiches

4 to 5 lbs. beef roast
12 oz. Coca-Cola
1 C. ketchup

1 (1 oz.) pkg. dry onion soup mix
15 hamburger buns

Spray a large slow cooker with nonstick cooking spray; add roast. In a small bowl, combine Coca-Cola, ketchup and soup mix; pour mixture over roast. Cook on high setting for 6 hours, stirring occasionally. Using two forks, shred roast. Serve on buns. Makes 15 servings.

Cola Roast

3 to 3½ lbs. beef roast*
1 (10.7 oz.) can cream of
   mushroom soup

12 oz. Pepsi (not diet)
1 (1 oz.) pkg. dry onion soup mix

Spray a large slow cooker with nonstick cooking spray; add roast. In a medium bowl, stir together cream of mushroom soup and Pepsi; pour over roast. Sprinkle with dry onion soup mix. Cook on low setting for 8 to 10 hours. Makes 6 to 8 servings.

Roast can be added when still partially frozen.

Glazed Ham

1 (5 lb.) ham*
1 (.62 oz.) container whole cloves
2¼ C. brown sugar
12 oz. Coca-Cola

1 (20 oz.) can pineapple rings, drained, juice reserved
1 C. sweet concord grape wine
10 to 12 maraschino cherries, optional

Preheat oven to 325°. With a sharp knife, score ham crosswise and lengthwise about 1″ apart and ¼″ deep. Stud ham with cloves. Place ham in an aluminum roasting pan set on a baking sheet. Sprinkle brown sugar on top of ham. Bake for 20 to 30 minutes or until sugar begins to melt. Remove from oven and pour Coca-Cola over the ham, basting with sugar mixture in pan. Return to oven and bake for an additional 20 minutes. In a 2-cup glass measuring cup, stir together pineapple juice and wine. Pour slowly over ham. Return to oven and bake for an additional 15 minutes per pound of ham, basting every 20 minutes with juice in pan. During the last 20 minutes of baking time, add pineapple rings and cherries to ham, securing in place with toothpicks as needed. Makes 10 to 15 servings.

Do not use a glazed spiral-cut ham.

Soda Pop Chops

1 T. vegetable oil
6 pork chops
1 onion, sliced
12 oz. Coca-Cola
3 T. prepared mustard

⅓ C. ketchup
Black pepper to taste
Garlic powder to taste
1 (8 oz.) can mushrooms

Heat oil in a large skillet over medium heat. Brown both sides of pork chops; drain and remove from skillet. In same skillet, fry onion until tender; remove from skillet. In same skillet, stir together Coca-Cola, mustard, ketchup, black pepper, garlic powder and mushrooms. Place pork chops and onion back into skillet along with Coca-Cola mixture. Cover and simmer on low heat for 30 to 45 minutes or until sauce is thickened and pork chops are cooked to desired doneness. Makes 6 servings.

Baked Pork Chops

24 oz. Dr. Pepper
1 C. brown sugar
1 tsp. garlic powder
2 tsp. ground cloves
½ tsp. ground ginger

1 tsp. black pepper
1 tsp. salt
1 onion, sliced
6 center-cut pork chops

Preheat oven to 325°. In a 9 x 13″ baking pan, stir together Dr. Pepper, brown sugar, garlic powder, cloves, ginger, black pepper, salt and onion. Bake for 15 minutes; stir. Add pork chops to pan with Dr. Pepper mixture; cover with aluminum foil. Bake for 3 hours. Makes 6 servings.

Orange-Glazed Pork Loin

4 lbs. pork roast
1 C. Dr. Pepper
½ C. orange marmalade

¼ C. soy sauce
2 T. ground ginger

Preheat oven to 325°. Cut several ½″ deep slits in pork roast and place fat side up in a shallow baking pan. In a small bowl, whisk together Dr. Pepper, marmalade, soy sauce and ginger. Brush mixture over pork roast. Cover and bake, basting occasionally, for 2 hours or until the internal temperature reaches 160° to 170°. Remove from oven and let stand for 20 minutes before carving. Makes 10 servings.

Marinated Pork Loin

½ C. soy sauce	1 tsp. ground ginger
½ C. Coca-Cola	1 tsp. dried thyme
2 cloves garlic, minced	4 to 5 lbs. boned pork loin roast,
1 T. dry mustard	rolled and tied

In a small bowl, combine soy sauce, Coca-Cola, garlic, dry mustard, ginger and thyme. Place roast in a large resealable plastic bag and set it in a deep bowl. Pour marinade over roast and seal bag. Refrigerate overnight, turning bag several times. Preheat oven to 325°. Remove roast and place on a rack in a shallow roasting pan. Bake uncovered for 2½ to 3 hours or until a meat thermometer registers 160° to 170°. Pour marinade in a small saucepan and bring to a boil. Baste roast occasionally with marinade during the last hour of baking time. Makes 8 to 15 servings.

Citrus-Glazed Pork Tenderloin

3 T. olive oil
1 lb. pork tenderloin, cut into 1″ cubes
2 large potatoes, cut into 1″ cubes
1 C. chopped onion
2 poblano peppers, seeded
    and chopped

1 red bell pepper, seeded and chopped
1 tsp. salt
2 T. flour
2 C. orange juice
2 C. Pepsi

Heat oil in a Dutch oven or heavy skillet over high heat. Add tenderloin and potatoes; sauté for 4 minutes or until golden brown. Add onion, poblano peppers and bell pepper. Continue cooking for 3 to 5 minutes or until onion is translucent. Sprinkle tenderloin and vegetables with salt and flour; stir for 1 to 2 minutes. Add orange juice and Pepsi. Reduce heat to a simmer. Cover and cook for 40 to 50 minutes or until liquid has reduced and thickened. Makes 4 servings.

Slow Cooker Jerk Sandwiches

1 T. dry Jamaican jerk seasoning
12½ lb. boneless pork shoulder, trimmed
¼ tsp. dried thyme
½ C. chopped onion

1 C. Pepsi
2 C. barbeque sauce
8 sandwich buns or 10″ flour tortillas

Spray a 3½- to 4-quart slow cooker with nonstick cooking spray. Rub jerk seasoning over pork and sprinkle with thyme. Place pork in slow cooker. Sprinkle with onion. Pour Pepsi over all. Cover; cook on low setting for 8 to 10 hours. Remove pork from slow cooker. Reserve ½ cup juice; discard remaining juice. Using two forks, shred pork. Return pork to slow cooker. Stir in barbeque sauce and reserved juice. Cover and cook on high setting for 30 to 45 minutes or until thoroughly heated. Serve on buns. Makes 8 servings.

Smoked Sausages

1 (24 oz.) bottle ketchup
1 to 2 C. brown sugar, divided
12 oz. Pepsi

2 (16 oz.) pkgs. miniature
smoked sausages

In a slow cooker, combine ketchup, 1 cup brown sugar and Pepsi; mix well. Stir in sausages. Cook on high setting for 1 hour; reduce to low setting and cook for an additional 2 hours. Add remaining 1 cup brown sugar, if desired. Makes 6 to 8 servings.

Pepsi Chicken & Rice

4 boneless, skinless chicken breast
   halves, cut into bite-size pieces
2 C. uncooked rice

1 to 2 C. barbeque sauce
1 to 2 C. Pepsi (not diet)

Preheat oven to 250°. In a large skillet, cook chicken until no longer pink. Spray a 9 x 13″ baking pan with nonstick cooking spray. Pour rice evenly into prepared pan and place chicken over rice. In a medium bowl, whisk together barbeque sauce and Pepsi. Pour half the barbeque sauce mixture over chicken in pan. Cover and bake for 3 to 5 hours, stirring in more barbeque sauce mixture throughout baking time as needed to keep rice moist. Makes 4 servings.

Baked Pepsi Chicken

3 lbs. boneless, skinless chicken
    breast halves
1 (10.7 oz.) can cream of onion soup
1 (10.7 oz.) can cream of
    mushroom soup

12 oz. Diet Pepsi
1 tsp. dried parsley
Salt and black pepper to taste
Cooked rice, optional

Preheat oven to 350°. Spray a 9 x 13″ baking pan with nonstick cooking spray. Slice chicken into wide strips and place in prepared pan. In a medium bowl, whisk together cream of onion soup, cream of mushroom soup and Diet Pepsi. Pour over chicken in pan and sprinkle with parsley. Bake for 30 to 45 minutes or until chicken is done. Serve over rice, if desired. Makes 6 servings.

Orange Soda Chicken

1½ lbs. boneless, skinless chicken
    breast halves

12 oz. orange soda
½ C. soy sauce

Place chicken in a slow cooker. In a 2-cup measuring cup, stir together orange soda and soy sauce. Pour over chicken in slow cooker. Cook on low setting for 5 to 6 hours or until chicken is done. Makes 3 to 4 servings.

BBQ Chicken

1 C. ketchup
12 oz. Diet Pepsi
2 tsp. cider vinegar
¼ tsp. hot pepper sauce

⅔ C. chopped onion
4 boneless, skinless chicken
    breast halves

In a large skillet over medium-high heat, stir together ketchup, Diet Pepsi, vinegar, hot pepper sauce and onion. Add chicken and bring to a boil; cover. Reduce heat to a simmer and cook for 50 minutes or until chicken is fork tender and no longer pink. Makes 4 servings.

Garlicky Chicken Wings

1 T. olive oil
1½ lbs. chicken wings
¾ C. Coca-Cola

2½ T. soy sauce
½ C. brown sugar
Garlic powder to taste

Heat oil in a large skillet over medium heat. Add chicken and fry until browned on both sides. In a small bowl, whisk together Coca-Cola, soy sauce, brown sugar and garlic powder; pour over wings in skillet. Reduce heat to low; cover and cook for 30 minutes, turning occasionally. Remove cover and cook for an additional 15 minutes or until sauce thickens. Makes 4 servings.

Foiled Fish For One

6 oz. halibut steak

4 medium fresh mushrooms, halved

2 cherry tomatoes, halved

2 lemon slices

½ green bell pepper, seeded and sliced

¼ C. Diet Sprite

Salt and black pepper to taste

Preheat oven to 375°. Spray a 20″ length of aluminum foil with nonstick cooking spray. Place fish in the middle of foil and add mushrooms, tomatoes, lemon slices and bell pepper. Fold up edges of foil and slowly add Sprite. Tightly seal edges to form a packet. Bake for 20 to 25 minutes or until fish flakes easily. Carefully open foil and sprinkle with salt and black pepper. Makes 1 serving.

Sweet & Sour Salmon

12 oz. Coca-Cola
1½ T. balsamic vinegar
1¼ tsp. salt, divided
½ C. pearl onions
½ C. bias-cut parsnips
½ C. bias-cut carrots

¼ C. snow peas, strings removed
1 T. olive oil, divided
1¼ lb. salmon fillet, skin on
½ tsp. black pepper
1¼ C. white button mushrooms,
   trimmed and sliced

In a large saucepan over medium-high heat, whisk together Coca-Cola, vinegar and a pinch of salt. Cook for 20 minutes or until liquid is reduced to ½ cup; remove from heat and set aside. In a medium saucepan over medium heat, combine onions, parsnips and carrots. Cover with water and heat to boiling. Boil for 5 minutes; add snow peas. Continue boiling for an additional 2 to 3 minutes; drain and set aside. Meanwhile, heat 2 teaspoons oil in a large nonstick skillet over medium heat. Season salmon fillets with 1 teaspoon salt and black pepper. Place fillets skin side down into skillet. Sauté for 5 to 7 minutes or until golden brown. Flip fish and sauté until opaque but still tender,

continued on next page

about 5 minutes. Remove from skillet; keep warm. In the same skillet, heat remaining 1 teaspoon oil over medium heat; stir in mushrooms, 1½ teaspoons water and a pinch of salt. Cook for 2 to 3 minutes or until just tender. Add onions, parsnips, carrots and snow peas; stir to combine and heat through. Serve fillets and mixed vegetables drizzled with Coca-Cola mixture. Makes 4 servings.

Breaded Fish Fillets

½ C. Mountain Dew
½ C. cornstarch
½ C. dried bread crumbs

Salt and black pepper to taste
2 T. vegetable oil
1½ lbs. fish fillets

Pour Mountain Dew into a shallow dish. In a separate shallow dish, stir together cornstarch, bread crumbs, salt and pepper. Heat oil in a large skillet over medium heat until very hot. Dip both sides of fish fillets into Mountain Dew, then dip both sides into cornstarch mixture. Carefully place in hot oil. Fry on one side until crispy and brown. Flip fish and fry until the other side is crispy and brown. Drain on a paper towel-lined plate. Makes 4 servings.

Desserts

Pineapple Empanadas

1 (10 to 16 oz.) jar pineapple preserves
4 to 5 T. cornstarch
½ C. sugar
6 C. flour

2 C. butter-flavored shortening
1 to 1¼ C. Coca-Cola, room
   temperature
Powdered sugar for sprinkling

Preheat oven to 350°. Spray a baking sheet with nonstick cooking spray; set aside. In a medium saucepan over medium heat, stir together preserves, cornstarch and sugar. Bring to a boil; set aside. In a large bowl, combine flour and shortening with a pastry blender or two knives until mixture is crumbly and well combined. Slowly add Coca-Cola until dough forms a ball. Divide dough into balls about 2″ in diameter. Roll each ball into a flat disc. Spread each disc with a portion of the pineapple mixture to within ½″ of edge. Fold in half and pinch edges to seal. Bake on prepared baking sheet for 15 to 18 minutes or until lightly browned. Remove from oven and immediately sprinkle with powdered sugar. Makes 48 servings.

Lemon Cheesecake with a Twist

2 C. graham cracker crumbs
½ C. powdered sugar
1 tsp. ground cinnamon
½ C. butter, melted
1 (.25 oz.) pkg. unflavored gelatin
1½ C. 7UP, divided
1 (3 oz.) pkg. lemon cook-and-serve
   pudding mix

6 T. sugar
2 eggs, beaten
11 oz. cream cheese, softened
½ C. strawberry jelly
½ pt. fresh strawberries, sliced

Spray a 9″ springform pan with nonstick cooking spray; set aside. In a medium bowl, combine cracker crumbs, powdered sugar, cinnamon and butter; mix well. Press into the bottom and 2″ up the sides of prepared pan; chill. In a small bowl, stir together gelatin and ¼ cup 7UP; let stand for 4 minutes. Meanwhile, in a medium saucepan over medium heat, stir together pudding mix, sugar, eggs and ¾ cup water. Add remaining 1¼ cups 7UP and bring just to a boil, stirring constantly; remove from
continued on next page

continued on next page

heat. Stir in softened gelatin; cool for 3 minutes. In a medium mixing bowl, add ½ cup gelatin mixture to cream cheese and beat on medium speed with an electric mixer until smooth. Add remaining gelatin mixture and mix until well blended. Pour into chilled crust and chill overnight. Remove sides from pan. In a small microwave-safe dish, heat jelly in microwave until melted. Brush half the melted jelly over cheesecake and top with sliced strawberries; pour remaining jelly over the top. Makes 12 servings.

Citrus Baked Apples

4 baking apples
¼ C. raisins

¼ C. brown sugar
½ C. Squirt

Preheat oven to 350°. Remove core of each apple without cutting through the bottom, creating a cavity in each. Stand apples in an 8 x 8″ baking dish. Place 1 tablespoon raisins and 1 tablespoon brown sugar inside each apple. Pour Squirt into and around apples in pan. Bake for 45 minutes, basting frequently, or until apples are tender but not mushy. Serve warm or chilled. Makes 4 servings.

Cherry Cobbler

2 (21 oz.) cans cherry pie filling   12 oz. 7UP
1 (18.2 oz.) pkg. yellow cake mix

Preheat oven to 350°. Spray a 9 x 13″ baking pan with nonstick cooking spray. Pour pie filling into pan and sprinkle with dry cake mix. Pour 7UP over cake mix in pan. Bake for 45 minutes or until set. Makes 12 servings.

Apple Cobbler

2 (8 oz.) tubes refrigerated crescent
    roll dough
2 Granny Smith apples, peeled, each
    cut into 8 pieces
1 C. butter

1½ C. sugar
12 oz. Mountain Dew
Ground cinnamon, optional
Chopped pecans, optional

Preheat oven to 350°. Spray a 9 x 13″ baking pan with nonstick cooking spray; set aside. Divide crescent roll dough into triangles. Place an apple piece on each triangle; roll up from short end, wrapping apple in dough. Place each apple-filled crescent roll in prepared pan. In a small saucepan over low heat, melt butter; add sugar, stirring until sugar dissolves. Pour butter mixture evenly over crescent rolls in pan. Slowly pour Mountain Dew over crescent rolls in pan. Sprinkle with cinnamon and chopped pecans, if desired. Bake, uncovered, for about 45 minutes or until crescent rolls are brown. Makes 16 servings.

Orange Angel Puffs

½ C. diet orange soda*   1 (16 oz.) pkg. angel food cake mix
¼ tsp. almond extract

Preheat oven to 350°. Spray a baking sheet with nonstick cooking spray; set aside. In a large mixing bowl, beat together orange soda, almond extract and cake mix. Drop batter by heaping tablespoonfuls on prepared baking sheet. Bake for 9 minutes or until lightly browned. Remove from oven; immediately remove from baking sheets and place on a wire rack to cool. Makes 14 puffs.

*Try with strawberry soda or 7UP.

Lemon Bars

1 (18.2 oz.) pkg. confetti or white
   cake mix
12 oz. Diet Mountain Dew
1 (3.4 oz.) pkg. lemon instant
   pudding mix

2 C. milk
1 (8 oz.) container whipped
   topping, thawed

Preheat oven to 350°. Spray a 9 x 13″ baking pan with nonstick cooking spray; set aside. In a medium bowl, stir together cake mix and Diet Mountain Dew. Spread evenly in prepared pan. Bake for 25 to 30 minutes. Remove from oven and cool on a wire rack. In a medium bowl, whisk together pudding mix and milk until well combined and thickened. Refrigerate until chilled. Spread pudding evenly over cooled bars. Spread whipped topping evenly over pudding. Makes 18 to 24 servings.

Applesauce Brownies

1½ C. butter, softened, divided
3 oz. semi-sweet baking chocolate
2 C. sugar
3 eggs
1 C. applesauce

2 C. flour
3 T. unsweetened cocoa powder
6 T. Coca-Cola
3¾ C. powdered sugar

Preheat oven to 350°. Spray a 9 x 13" baking pan with nonstick cooking spray; set aside. In a large microwave-safe bowl, combine 1 cup butter and baking chocolate. Microwave uncovered on high power until melted. Stir in sugar, eggs, applesauce and flour until well combined. Pour mixture into prepared pan. Bake for 25 to 30 minutes or until a toothpick inserted in center of brownies comes out clean. Remove from oven and set on a wire rack. Meanwhile, in a medium saucepan, melt remaining ½ cup butter; stir in cocoa powder and Coca-Cola. Add powdered sugar, stirring until smooth. Spread over hot brownies. Makes 18 to 24 servings.

Brownies

2 C. sugar
2 C. flour
4 eggs
1 C. butter, melted

½ C. unsweetened cocoa powder, divided
1 tsp. vanilla extract
1 C. chopped pecans

Preheat oven to 350°. Spray a 9 x 13″ baking pan with nonstick cooking spray; set aside. In a large mixing bowl, combine sugar, flour, eggs, butter, cocoa powder, vanilla and pecans with an electric mixer on medium speed; beat for 2 minutes. Pour mixture into prepared pan. Bake for 25 to 30 minutes or until a toothpick inserted in center of brownies comes out clean. Remove from oven and set on a wire rack. While brownies are warm, frost with Chocolate Cola Icing, page 94. Makes 18 to 24 servings.

Chocolate Cola Cupcakes

1¾ C. flour
2 C. sugar
¾ C. unsweetened cocoa powder, sifted
2 tsp. baking soda
1 tsp. baking powder
Pinch of salt

1 tsp. vanilla extract
2 eggs
½ C. vegetable oil
1 C. Coca-Cola
1 C. buttermilk

Preheat oven to 350°. Place paper liners in two 12-cup muffin pans; set aside. In a large bowl, stir together flour, sugar, cocoa powder, baking soda, baking powder and salt. Whisk in vanilla, eggs, oil, Coca-Cola and buttermilk until well combined. Pour mixture into prepared pans. Bake for 20 to 24 minutes or until a toothpick inserted in center of cupcakes comes out clean. Frost with Chocolate Cola Icing, page 94. Makes 18 to 24 servings.

Chocolate Cola Icing

½ C. butter
¼ C. unsweetened cocoa powder
⅓ C. Coca-Cola

3 C. powdered sugar
½ tsp. vanilla extract
1 C. chopped pecans, optional

In a medium saucepan over medium heat, stir together butter, cocoa powder and Coca-Cola until butter melts. Remove from heat. Gradually stir in powdered sugar and vanilla until smooth and creamy. Stir in pecans, if desired. Frosts 1 cake.

Chocolate-Covered Cherries Cake

1 (10 oz.) jar maraschino cherries, drained, ¼ C. juice reserved
1 (18.2 oz.) pkg. devil's food cake mix
1 C. Wild Cherry Pepsi
½ C. vegetable oil
3 eggs

1 (12 oz.) container whipped vanilla frosting
1 C. marshmallow creme
24 maraschino cherries with stems, well drained, optional

Preheat oven to 350°. Spray a 9 x 13″ baking pan with nonstick cooking spray; set aside. Chop drained maraschino cherries; set aside. In a large mixing bowl, beat together cake mix, Wild Cherry Pepsi, oil, eggs and reserved cherry juice with an electric mixer on low speed for 30 seconds. Beat on medium speed for 2 minutes. Stir in chopped cherries. Pour into prepared pan. Bake for 35 to 45 minutes or until a toothpick inserted in center of cake comes out clean; cool completely. In a small bowl, mix together frosting and marshmallow creme until smooth. Frost cake. Top each piece with a stemmed cherry. Makes 18 to 24 servings.

Root Beer Float Cake

1 (18.2 oz.) pkg. white cake mix
2 eggs
1¾ C. root beer, chilled, divided

¼ C. vegetable oil
1 (1.3 oz.) pkg. whipped topping mix

Preheat oven to 350°. Spray a 9 x 13″ baking pan with nonstick cooking spray; set aside. In a large mixing bowl, beat together cake mix, eggs, 1¼ cups root beer and oil with an electric mixer on low speed for 30 seconds. Beat on high speed for 2 minutes. Pour into prepared pan and bake for 35 to 40 minutes; cool in pan on a wire rack. In a small mixing bowl, beat whipped topping mix and remaining ½ cup root beer with an electric mixer on high speed until stiff peaks form. Spread over cooled cake; chill before serving. Makes 24 servings.

Strawberry Soda Cake

1 (18.2 oz.) pkg. white cake mix
Water, eggs and oil as directed
    on package
1 (3 oz.) pkg. strawberry gelatin
12 oz. strawberry soda*

1 (5.2 oz.) pkg. vanilla instant
    pudding mix
1½ C. milk
1 (8 oz.) container whipped topping,
    thawed

Preheat oven to 350°. Spray a 9 x 13″ baking pan with nonstick cooking spray; set aside. Combine cake mix, water, eggs and oil as directed on package. Bake according to directions on package. Remove cake from oven and poke holes in cake with a fork. In a medium bowl, combine 1½ cups boiling water and strawberry gelatin, stirring until dissolved. Whisk in strawberry soda. Pour mixture slowly over cake, allowing liquid to soak in. Refrigerate cake until cool. In a medium bowl, combine pudding mix and milk. Beat until well blended and thickened. Fold in whipped topping. Spread on cake. Refrigerate several hours. Makes 18 to 24 servings.

*Try using cream soda.

7UP Bundt Cake

1½ C. butter, softened
3 C. sugar
5 eggs
3 C. flour

2 T. lemon flavoring
¾ C. 7UP
⅔ C. powdered sugar
1 T. lemon juice

Preheat oven to 325°. Spray a 10″ Bundt pan with nonstick cooking spray; set aside. In a large mixing bowl, beat together butter and sugar with an electric mixer for 2 to 3 minutes. Add eggs, one at a time, mixing well after each addition. Add flour and lemon flavoring; stir in 7UP. Pour into prepared pan. Bake for 1 hour and 20 minutes or until a toothpick inserted in center of the cake comes out clean. Cool completely. In a small bowl, stir together powdered sugar and lemon juice until smooth. Drizzle over cake. Makes 18 to 24 servings.

Pineapple 7UP Cake

1 (18.2 oz.) yellow cake mix
1 (3 oz.) pkg. pineapple instant
   pudding mix
½ C. vegetable oil
4 eggs
12 oz. 7UP
½ C. butter

1½ C. sugar
2 T. flour
2 egg yolks, slightly beaten
1 (8 oz.) can crushed pineapple,
   with juice
1 C. sweetened flaked coconut
1 C. chopped pecans

Preheat oven to 350°. Spray a 9 x 13″ baking pan with nonstick cooking spray; set aside. In a large bowl, stir together cake mix and pudding mix. Stir in oil until combined. Add eggs, one at a time, mixing well after each addition. Slowly add 7UP, stirring until well blended. Pour mixture into prepared pan and bake for 30 minutes or until a toothpick inserted in center of cake comes out clean. In a medium saucepan over medium heat, melt butter. Add sugar, flour, egg yolks and pineapple with juice. Cook, stirring constantly, until thickened. Stir in coconut and pecans. Spread evenly over cake; store in refrigerator. Makes 18 to 24 servings.

Dr. Pepper Cake

1 C. quick-cooking oats
1¼ C. Dr. Pepper
½ C. shortening
½ C. sugar
1 C. brown sugar

2 eggs
1⅓ C. flour
½ tsp. salt
1 tsp. baking soda
½ tsp. ground nutmeg

Preheat oven to 375°. Grease and flour a metal 9 x 9″ baking pan; set aside. Place oats in a small bowl. In a small saucepan, heat the Dr. Pepper to boiling and pour over oats; let stand for 15 to 20 minutes. Meanwhile, in a large mixing bowl, beat together shortening, sugar and brown sugar with an electric mixer on medium speed until well combined. Add eggs, beating until mixture is fluffy. Sift together flour, salt, baking soda and nutmeg; add to creamed mixture, mixing well. Add oatmeal mixture; mix thoroughly. Pour into prepared pan. Bake for 40 to 45 minutes or until a toothpick inserted in center of cake comes out clean. Frost immediately with Broiled Coconut Frosting, page 101.

Broiled Coconut Frosting

⅓ C. butter, melted
½ C. brown sugar

¼ C. half-and-half
1 C. sweetened flaked coconut

Preheat oven to broil. In a medium bowl, combine melted butter, brown sugar, half-and-half and coconut; mix well. Spread evenly over hot cake. Place briefly under the broiler until bubbly and lightly browned. Serve warm. Frosts 1 cake.

Coca-Cola Carrot Cake

3 eggs
2¼ C. sugar, divided
½ C. vegetable oil
¾ C. plus 6 T. Coca-Cola
2 tsp. vanilla extract, divided
2 C. flour, sifted
1 tsp. baking soda
½ tsp. salt

2 T. plus 2 tsp. unsweetened
    cocoa powder
2¼ C. grated carrots
1 C. chopped walnuts
1 C. sweetened flaked coconut
6 T. butter
1 T. light corn syrup

Preheat oven to 350°. Spray a 9 x 13″ baking pan with nonstick cooking spray; set aside. In a large mixing bowl, beat eggs with an electric mixer on medium speed until well combined. Add 1½ cups sugar, oil, ¾ cup Coca-Cola and 1½ teaspoons vanilla; beat well. In a medium bowl, stir together flour, baking soda, salt and 2 tablespoons cocoa powder. Add flour mixture to egg mixture, beating until smooth. Stir in carrots, walnuts and coconut until well combined. Pour into prepared pan and bake for 40 to

continued on next page

50 minutes or until a toothpick inserted in center of cake comes out clean. Remove from oven and poke holes in hot cake with the handle of a wooden spoon. In a small saucepan over low heat, combine butter, syrup, remaining ¾ cup sugar, 2 teaspoons cocoa powder and 6 tablespoons Coca-Cola. Bring to a boil, stirring constantly, for 5 minutes or until thick and syrupy. Stir in remaining ½ teaspoon vanilla. Remove from heat; pour syrup mixture evenly over hot cake. Serve warm or at room temperature. Makes 18 to 24 servings.

Orange Pound Cake

1¼ C. butter, softened, divided
½ C. shortening
2¾ C. sugar
5 eggs
3 C. cake flour
½ tsp. salt

1 C. orange soda
1 tsp. vanilla extract
1 T. plus 1 tsp. orange flavoring
1 (8 oz.) pkg. cream cheese, softened
3¾ C. powdered sugar

Preheat oven to 350°. Grease and flour a 10″ fluted tube pan; set aside. In a large mixing bowl, beat together 1 cup butter, shortening and sugar with an electric mixer on medium speed until fluffy. Add eggs, one at a time, beating well after each addition. In a small bowl, sift together flour and salt. Add to butter mixture, alternately with orange soda, vanilla and 1 tablespoon orange flavoring. Pour batter into prepared pan; bake for 1 hour 10 minutes or until cake is golden brown. Remove from oven; cool for 10 minutes. Remove cake from pan and cool completely on a wire rack. In a medium mixing bowl, beat remaining ¼ cup butter and cream cheese with an electric mixer on medium speed until smooth. Slowly add powdered sugar, beating until creamy. Stir in remaining 1 teaspoon orange flavoring. Spread over cooled cake. Makes 12 servings.

Mellow Yellow Cake

1 (18.2 oz.) pkg. lemon cake mix
Eggs and oil as directed on package
12 oz. Mellow Yellow
1 (8 oz.) can crushed pineapple, drained

½ C. butter
1 (14 oz.) can sweetened
    condensed milk
1 (7 oz.) bag sweetened flaked coconut

Preheat oven to 350°. Spray a 9 x 13″ baking pan with nonstick cooking spray; set aside. Combine cake mix, eggs and oil as directed on package, stirring in Mellow Yellow in place of water. Fold in pineapple. Bake according to directions until a toothpick inserted in the center of cake comes out clean. Remove from oven and place pan on a wire rack. Poke holes in warm cake with the handle of a wooden spoon. In a medium saucepan over low heat, combine butter, sweetened condensed milk and coconut, stirring until butter is melted and ingredients are well combined. Pour warm mixture over warm cake. Refrigerate for several hours or until cake is completely cool. Makes 18 to 24 servings.

Ice Cream Soda

Strawberry ice cream
Wild Cherry Pepsi
Root beer

Whipped topping, thawed
Maraschino cherries

Place 1 scoop ice cream into each of 4 soda glasses. Fill to half with Wild Cherry Pepsi. Add another scoop of ice cream; fill to nearly full with root beer. Top each with a dollop of whipped topping and a cherry. Makes 4 servings.

"Doctored-Up" Peanut Brittle

1½ C. sugar
¾ C. butter plus more for greasing pan
1½ tsp. salt

¼ C. Dr. Pepper
2 C. raw peanuts, shelled
½ tsp. baking soda

Grease a 10 x 15″ jellyroll pan with butter. In a large heavy saucepan, combine sugar, butter, salt, Dr. Pepper and peanuts. Bring to a boil over medium heat, stirring often. Boil until candy thermometer inserted into mixture reaches 290°. Remove pan from heat and stir in baking soda. Pour into greased pan. Allow to cool completely before breaking into pieces. Makes 1¾ pounds.

Index

Desserts